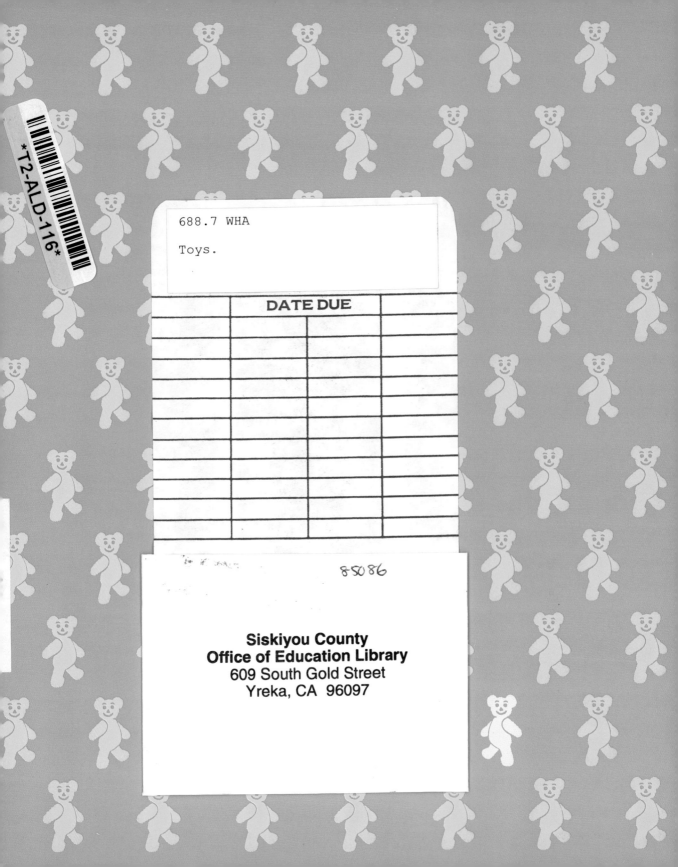

A Dorling Kindersley Book

Conceived, edited and designed by DK Direct Limited

Note to parents

What's Inside? Toys is designed to help young children understand how some of the most familiar toys work. It shows them how and why the propeller on a toy plane spins, what makes a doll cry when you squeeze her, and what makes a teddy bear growl. It is a book for you and your child to read and talk about together, and to enjoy.

Designers   Juliette Norsworthy and Sonia Whillock
Typographic Designer   Nigel Coath
Editors   Simon Bell and Alexandra Parsons
Design Director   Ed Day
Editorial Director   Jonathan Reed

Illustrator   Richard Manning
Photographers   Steve Gorton, Paul Bricknell and Michael Dunning
Writer   Angela Royston

A Scholastic Book Club Edition
First American Edition, 1991
Dorling Kindersley Inc., New York

Library of Congress Catalog Card Number: 91-60534

ISBN 0-590-45533-8

Printed in Italy

WHAT'S INSIDE?

TOYS

A SCHOLASTIC BOOK CLUB EDITION

DK

DORLING KINDERSLEY
NEW YORK

TEDDY BEAR

Here is a growling teddy bear. His name is Avalon.
He is nearly one hundred years old so no one plays
with him any more. He lives in a museum where he is
looked after very carefully.

Avalon looks like
a real-life bear
He has a long, pointed
nose and brown fur.

Avalon's nose
and eyes are made
of soft leather.

His fur is made of
mohair, a kind of
wool that comes
from goats.

Avalon's legs
and arms can all move.

When you turn Avalon
upside down and then
back again he growls,
just like a real bear.

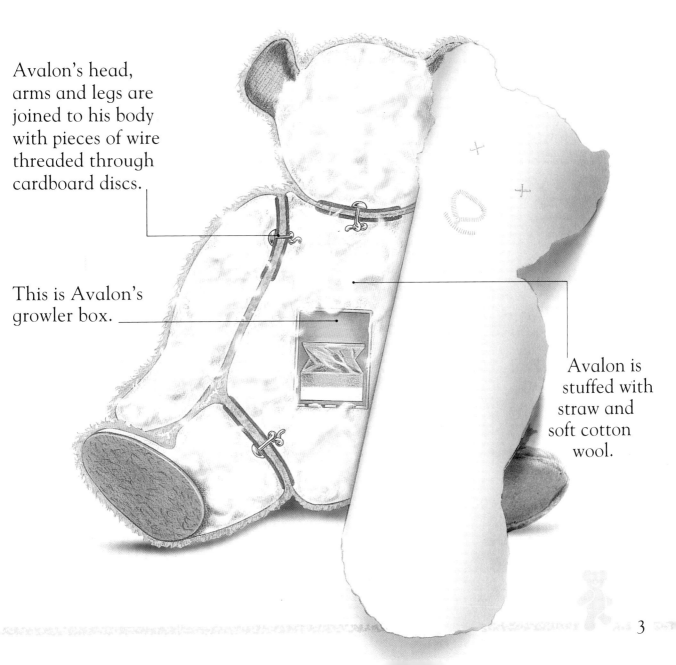

Avalon's head,
arms and legs are
joined to his body
with pieces of wire
threaded through
cardboard discs.

This is Avalon's
growler box.

Avalon is
stuffed with
straw and
soft cotton
wool.

AIRPLANE

The engine on this toy plane is a rubber band.
You turn the propeller round and round with your finger
to wind it up. When you let go, the propeller spins very fast
and the plane flies off through the air.

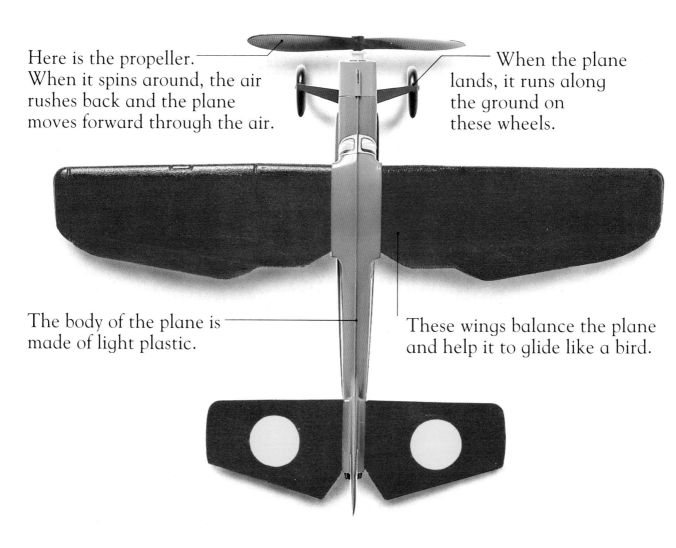

Here is the propeller.
When it spins around, the air
rushes back and the plane
moves forward through the air.

When the plane
lands, it runs along
the ground on
these wheels.

The body of the plane is
made of light plastic.

These wings balance the plane
and help it to glide like a bird.

The propeller spins so fast that you can only see a blur.

The wings are slotted through holes in the body.

The rubber band twists up tight when you wind the propeller.

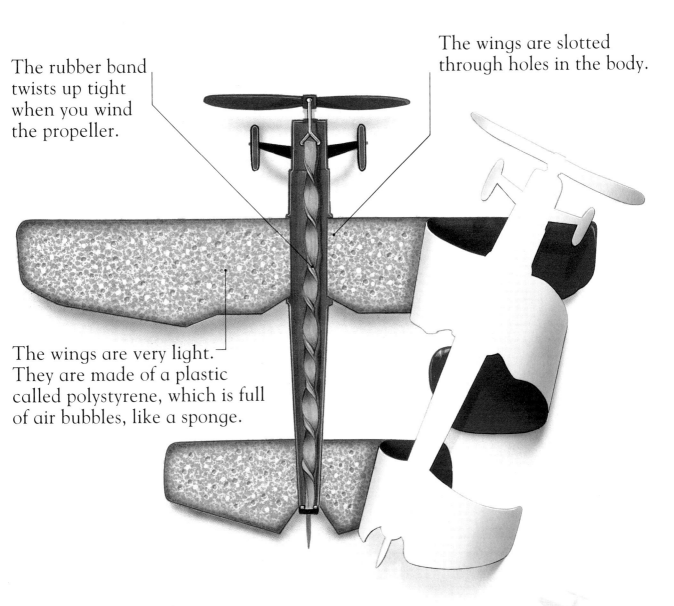

The wings are very light. They are made of a plastic called polystyrene, which is full of air bubbles, like a sponge.

JACK-IN-THE-BOX

When the box is closed, everything is quiet.
Open the box and out springs Jack.
Children have been playing
with these toys for more than
a hundred years, ever since
steel springs were invented.

Jack's box
is made of
painted wood.

Jack's head is heavy,
and it wobbles
from side to side.

This bell
on his hat
jingles as he
springs out.

His eyes and mouth
are painted on.

He is dressed
in a striped suit
like a circus clown.

This brass
clasp keeps
the box closed.

This little ball inside
the bell makes it jingle.

When Jack
is inside, his
body is squeezed
up tight.

Jack's head
is made of
heavy clay.

His hat is
stuffed with
cotton wool.

His hands
and arms
are made of
soft felt.

When you open
the lid the spring
stretches and
up pops Jack!

DOLLS' HOUSE

This dolls' house has been made to look like a house built nearly two hundred years ago. The front of the house opens like a cupboard to show all the treasures inside.

In a real house, smoke from an open fire or stove goes up the chimneys.

These are windows for the rooms in the attic, under the roof.

The walls, roof and window frames are all made of painted wood.

The window panes are made of clear plastic.

The front door of the house opens and closes.

The rooms have been decorated with wallpaper, pictures and carpets, just like a real house.

These hinges let the front of the house swing open.

The furniture looks like real furniture, only smaller.

The stairs in the house go all the way from the bottom to the top.

ROBOT

Zak the robot works on battery power. When you switch him on he makes a loud whirring noise, lights flash and off he marches. Left! Right! Left! Right!

This panel opens up. His chest moves forward and two lights flash yellow.

Zak's head and body whizz round and round as he marches along.

These grippers are made of metal.

Zak's body armor is made of tough plastic.

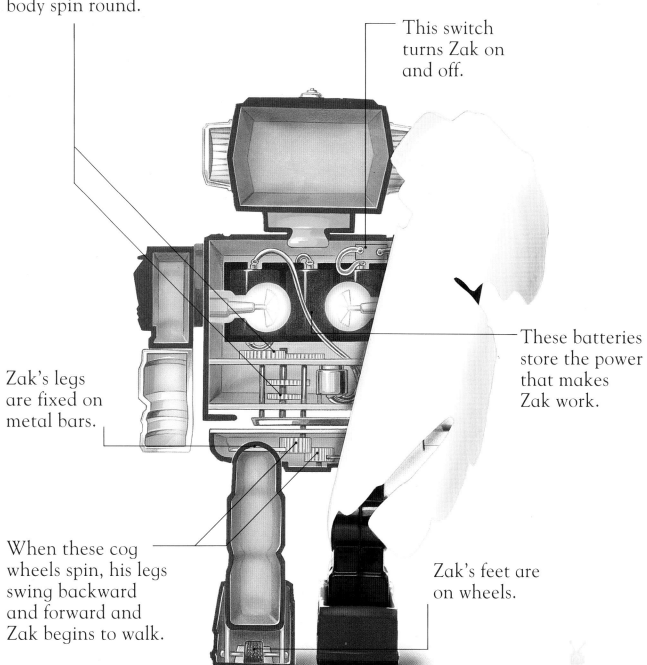

These cog-wheels spin the turntable that makes Zak's body spin round.

This switch turns Zak on and off.

These batteries store the power that makes Zak work.

Zak's legs are fixed on metal bars.

When these cog wheels spin, his legs swing backward and forward and Zak begins to walk.

Zak's feet are on wheels.

KALEIDOSCOPE

Look into the kaleidoscope and you will see a beautiful pattern.
As you turn the tube the pattern changes again and again.
The first kaleidoscopes were made two hundred years ago.

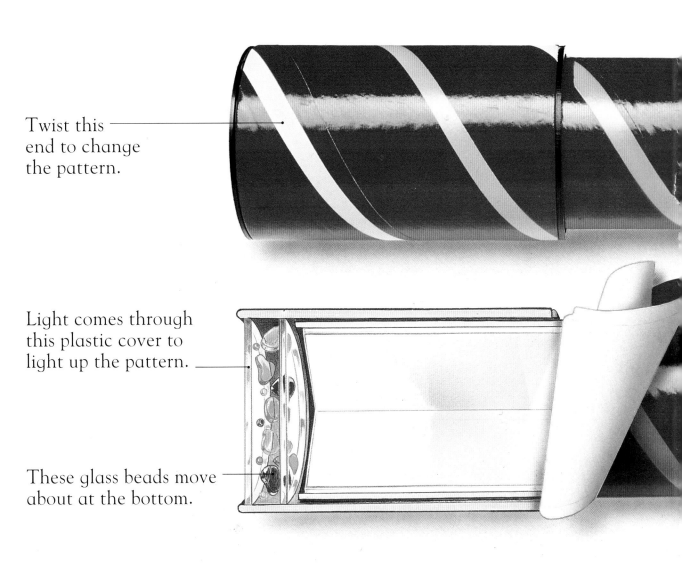

Twist this end to change the pattern.

Light comes through this plastic cover to light up the pattern.

These glass beads move about at the bottom.

The real beads are in this triangle.

This is a reflection of the beads in one of the mirrors.

This is a reflection of the reflection.

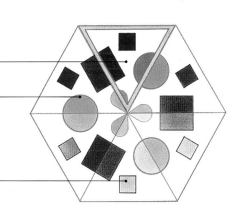

The outer tube is made of cardboard covered in brightly colored paper.

Three long mirrors make a triangle shape so that they reflect each other.

This is the hole that you look through.

DOLL

This doll is called Jennifer. She looks like a baby girl and her clothes are just like real baby clothes. She can even drink from a bottle and cry watery tears.

Jennifer's body is made of plastic. You can bath and dry her.

Her eyes open when she sits up and close when she lies down.

This is her bottle. When you put it in her mouth she drinks from it.

Her arms, legs and head all move.

The plastic used to make Jennifer is soft and warm to touch. She almost feels like a real baby!

When you squeeze her belly the water goes up these tubes to her eyes and she cries.

Jennifer's hair is threaded through tiny holes in her head.

Water from her baby bottle goes down into this tank in her belly.

When you squeeze this air sac, it pushes the water along the tear tubes.

PARTY FAVOR

Party favors are for birthdays and special occasions.
Grab hold of each end and pull. The favor bangs
and tears apart, and all the surprises tumble out.

The favor is covered in
thin, stretchy paper
that tears easily.

The banger strip is in
two parts. The bit where
they meet is coated with
explosive. Bang!

What's in this party favor?
Inside you will find a dice,
a whistle, a plastic bird
and a riddle or a joke.

This picture is glued on
to decorate the favor.

Hold this bit
tightly between your
thumb and finger
when you pull.

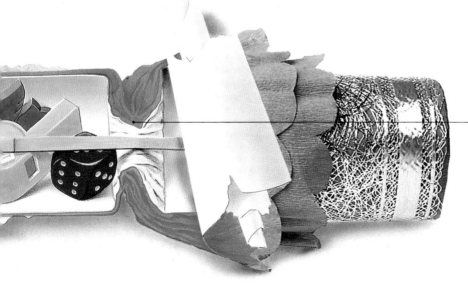

The paper is twisted
to make a handle
at each end.